Air Fryer Cookbook

For Beginners

Breakfast Recipes

For A Healthy Weight Loss

(Includes Alphabetic Index, Nutritional Facts

And Some Low Carb Recipes)

By

Barbara Trisler

www.MillenniumPublishingLimited.com

Copyright ©2019

Disclaimer

This publication is designed to provide competent and reliable information regarding the subject matter covered. However, it is sold with the understanding that the author is not engaged in rendering medical or other professional advice. Laws and practices often vary from state to state and country to country and if medical or other expert assistance is required, the services of a professional should be sought. The author specifically disclaims any liability that is incurred from the use or application of the contents of this book.

Table of Contents

What Is This Book All About?

This book contains proven steps and strategies on how to start preparing healthy and delicious meals that you can serve any time of the day using only one appliance – *the Air Fryer*. This innovation makes it possible to enjoy fried foods with less oil. You can also use it to whip up a wide range of dishes, snacks, and desserts.

It features loads of recipes that you can tweak in many ways to suit your preference and the availability of ingredients. Each recipe has a nutrient content guide per serving. In addition, it explains the basics about the appliance and the benefits of using it as compared to the traditional manner of frying food.

Finally, it also contains a quick guide of measurement conversion that can become handy when preparing your ingredients.

Please Note - There are two different version of this book – one with pictures and another without pictures. This particular version has *no pictures*. This is because of the prohibitive cost of printing images in color.

However, do not worry. A separate PDF recipe image booklet is available for download. It shows each recipe in this book in full color. To download it, go to *www.MillenniumPublishingLimited.com > Barbara Trisler > Air Fryer Cookbook Recipe Image Booklet.*

Without further ado, lets get started!

What is An Air Fryer?

An air fryer utilizes the convection mechanism in cooking food. It circulates hot air through the use of a mechanical fan to cook the ingredients inside the fryer. ***The process eliminates the use of too much oil*** in the traditional way of frying but still cooks food via the Maillard effect (i.e. a chemical reaction between an amino acid and a reducing sugar, usually requiring the addition of heat).

The process was named after the person who first explained it in 1912, French chemist Louis-Camille Maillard. The effect gives a distinctive flavor to browned foods, such as bread, biscuits, cookies, pan-fried meat, seared steaks, and many more.

The air fryer requires only a thin layer of oil for the ingredients to cook. It circulates hot air up to 392 degrees Fahrenheit. It's an innovative way of eliminating up to 80 percent of the oil that is traditionally used to fry different foods and prepare pastries.

You can find a dose of friendly features in air fryers depending on the brand you're using. Most brands include a timer adjustment and temperature control setting to make cooking easier and precise. An air fryer comes with a cooking basket where you'll place the food. The basket is placed on top of a drip tray. Depending on the model you're using, you will either be prompted to shake the basket to distribute oil evenly or it automatically does the job via a food agitator.

This is perfect for home use but if you're cooking for many people and you want to apply the same cooking technique, you can put your food items in specialized air crisper trays and cook them using a convection oven. An air fryer and convection oven apply the same technique in cooking but an air fryer has a smaller build and produces less heat.

How to Use Your Air Fryer

This appliance comes with a manual for easy assembly and as a handy guide for first-time users. Most brands also include a pamphlet of recipes to give you ideas about the wide range of dishes that you can create using this single kitchen appliance. Once you are ready to cook and you have all your ingredients ready, put them in the basket and insert it into the fryer. Other recipes will require you to preheat the air fryer before using. Once the basket is in, set the temperature and timer and begin cooking.

You can use an air fryer to cook food in a variety of ways. Once you get used with the basics, you can try its other features, such as advanced baking and using air fryer dehydrators.

Here are some of the cooking techniques that you can do with this single appliance:

- **Fry:** You can actually omit oil in cooking but a little amount adds crunch and flavor to your food. You can add oil to the ingredients while mixing or lightly spray the food with oil before cooking. You can use most kinds of oils but many users prefer peanut, olive, sunflower, and canola oils.
- **Roast:** You can produce the same quality of roasted foods like the ones cooked in a conventional roaster in a faster manner. This is recommended to people who need to come up with a special dish but do not have much time to prepare.
- **Bake:** There are baking pans suited for this appliance that you can use to bake bread, cookies, and other pastries. It only takes around 15 to 30 minutes to get your baked goodies done.
- **Grill:** It effectively grills your food easily and without mess. You only need to shake the basket halfway through the cooking process or flip the ingredients once or twice depending on the instructions. To make it easier, you can put the ingredients in a grill pan or grill layer with a handle, which other models include in the package or you can also buy one as an added accessory.

There are many kinds of foods that you can cook using an air fryer, but there are also certain types that are not suited for it. Avoid cooking ingredients, which can be steamed, like beans and carrots. You also cannot fry foods covered in heavy batter in this appliance.

Aside from the above mentioned, you can cook most kinds of ingredients using an air fryer. You can use it to cook foods covered in light flour or bread crumbs. You can cook a variety of vegetables in the appliance, such as cauliflower, asparagus, zucchini, kale, peppers, and corn on the cob. You can also use it to cook frozen foods and home prepared meals by following a different set of instructions for these purposes.

An air fryer also comes with another useful feature - the separator. It allows you to cook multiple dishes at a time. Use the separator to divide ingredients in the pan or basket. You have to make sure that all ingredients have the same temperature setting so that everything will cook evenly at the same time.

The Benefits of Air fryer

It is important to note that air fried foods are still fried. Unless you've decided to eliminate the use of oils in cooking, you must still be cautious about the food you eat. Despite that, it clearly presents a better and healthier option than deep frying. It helps you avoid unnecessary fats and oils, which makes it an ideal companion when you intend to lose weight. It offers a lot more benefits, which include the following:

- It is convenient and easy to use, plus, it's easy to clean.
- It doesn't give off unwanted smells when cooking.
- You can use it to prepare a variety of meals.
- It can withstand heavy cooking.
- It is durable and made of metal and high-grade plastic.
- Cooking using this appliance is not as messy as frying in a traditional way. You don't have to worry about greasy spills and stains in the kitchen.

Measurement Conversion Table

Measurement	Conversion
1 stick of butter	1/2 cup or 8 tablespoons
4 quarts	1 gallon
2 quarts	1/2 gallon

1 cup	8 fluid ounces or 1/2 pint or 16 tablespoons
2 cups	1 pint
1 quart	32 ounces or 2 pints or 4 cups
4 tablespoons	1/4 cup
8 tablespoons	1/2 cup
1/2 tablespoon	1 1/2 teaspoons
3 teaspoons	1 tablespoon

Breakfast Recipes

"The Bomb" Breakfast Balls

Nutritional Facts: Calories 305 Fat 15.0 g Protein 19.0 g Carbohydrates 26.0 g

Prep time: 20 min Cook time: 25 min

Servings: 2

Ingredients:

- Pizza dough, whole wheat, freshly prepared (4 ounces)
- Eggs, large, lightly beaten (3 pieces)
- Chives, fresh, chopped (1 tablespoon)
- Bacon slices, center cut (3 pieces)
- Cream cheese, 1/3-reduced-fat, softened (1 ounce)
- Cooking spray

Directions:

1. Cook the bacon over medium heat until crisp and browned. Crumble and set aside in a bowl.
2. Cook eggs in the bacon fat until almost set. Add eggs to the bowl filled with crumbled bacon. Stir along with the chives and cream cheese.
3. Cut pizza dough into four pieces, then roll to form 5-inch rounds. Fill each dough round with egg mixture (1/4 portion). Brush water on the edges before wrapping and pinching into a purse.
4. Add dough purses into the air fryer to cook for five minutes at 350 degrees Fahrenheit.

Scrumptious Sweet Potato Hash

Nutritional Facts: Calories 191 Fat 6.0 g Protein 3.7 g Carbohydrates 31.4 g

Prep Time: 10 min Cook time: 15 min

Servings: 6

Ingredients:

- Paprika, smoked (1 tablespoon)
- Bacon slices, chopped into tiny bits (2 pieces)
- Black pepper, freshly ground (1 teaspoon)
- Sweet potato, large, sliced into one-inch cubes (2 pieces)
- Olive oil, extra virgin (2 tablespoons)
- Sea salt (1 teaspoon)
- Dill weed, dried (1 teaspoon)

Directions:

1. Set the air fryer at 400 degrees Fahrenheit to preheat.
2. Combine the sweet potato with bacon, pepper, salt, olive oil, dill, and paprika.
3. Add the sweet potato mixture to the air fryer and cook for twelve to sixteen minutes.

Easy Hash Browns

Nutritional Facts: Calories 186 Fat 4.3 g Protein 4.0 g Carbohydrates 33.70 g

Prep Time: 15 min Cook time: 30 min

Servings: 4

Ingredients:

- Olive oil, extra virgin (1 tablespoon)
- Seasoning mix, taco (1/2 teaspoon)
- Jalapeno, w/ seeds removed, sliced into one-inch rings (1 piece)
- Salt (1/4 teaspoon)
- Black pepper, freshly ground (1/4 teaspoon)
- Potatoes, peeled, sliced into one-inch chunks (1 ½ pounds)
- Onion, small, sliced into one-inch chunks (1 piece)
- Olive oil, extra virgin (1/2 teaspoon)
- Cumin, ground (1/2 teaspoon)
- Bell pepper, red, w/ seeds removed, sliced into one-inch portions (1 piece)

Directions:

1. Let the potatoes sit in cold water for twenty minutes. Meanwhile, set the air fryer at 320 degrees Fahrenheit to preheat.
2. Drain, pat dry, and coat the potatoes with olive oil (1 tablespoon). Cook in the air fryer for eighteen minutes.
3. Toss the onion, jalapeno pepper, and bell pepper with olive oil (1/2 teaspoon), ground cumin, pepper, salt, and taco seasoning.
4. Combine the air-fried potatoes with the veggie mixture. Place in the air fryer and cook this time at 365 degrees Fahrenheit for ten minutes.

Doughnuts-To-Go

Nutritional Facts: Calories 238 Fat 4.0 g Protein 5.0 g Carbohydrates 46.0 g

Prep Time: 45 min Cook time: 35 min

Servings: 8

Ingredients:

- Tap water (4 teaspoons)
- Dry yeast, active (1 teaspoon)
- Sugar, powdered (1 cup)
- Milk, whole, at room temp. (1/4 cup)
- Flour, all purpose (2 cups)
- Egg, large, beaten (1 piece)
- Water, warmed to 100 to 100 degrees Fahrenheit (1/4 cup)
- Sugar, granulated, divided (1/4 cup + ½ teaspoon)
- Salt, kosher (1/4 teaspoon)
- Butter, unsalted, melted (2 tablespoons)

Directions:

1. Mix the yeast and granulated sugar (1/2 teaspoon) with water. Let stand to foam up.
2. Mix the remaining granulated sugar (1/4 cup) with salt and flour. Stir in the butter, egg, milk, and prepared yeast mixture to form a soft dough.
3. Knead the dough on a floured surface. Once smooth, place in a covered bowl and set aside to rise and double in size.
4. Roll the dough out until it is a quarter-of-an-inch-thick. Use a 3-inch circle cutter to make 8 rounds, then use a 1-inch circle cutter to cut out their centers. Let the 8 doughnuts and 8 doughnut holes rise, covered loosely, for half an hour on a floured surface.
5. Working in batches, cook the doughnut pieces in the air fryer for four to five minutes at 350 degrees Fahrenheit.

6. Whisk tap water and powdered sugar together to form a smooth glaze. Dip the doughnut pieces in the glaze, then let stand to allow the glaze to harden.

7. Serve and enjoy.

Breakfast Cheese Rolls

Nutritional Facts: Calories 97 Fat 5.5 g Protein 2.7 g Carbohydrates 9.2 g

Prep Time: 15 min Cook time: 10 min

Servings: 20

Ingredients:

- Manioc starch (3/4 cup)
- Salt (1 teaspoon)
- Water (1/4 cup)
- Cheddar cheese, shredded (3/4 cup)
- Manioc starch, sweet (3/4 cup)
- Milk, whole (1 /4 cup)
- Olive oil, extra virgin (1/4 cup)
- Eggs, beaten lightly (2 pieces)
- Parmigiano-Reggiano cheese, grated finely (1/2 cup)

Directions:

1. Set the air fryer at 325 degrees Fahrenheit to preheat.
2. Combine the sour manioc and sweet manioc starches.
3. Combine milk with salt, olive oil, and water, then heat until boiling. Lower heat before stirring in the starches. Keep stirring until you have an extremely dry mixture. Let cool.
4. Stir the eggs into the cooled starch mixture to form a smooth dough. Mix well with the Parmigiano-Reggiano and Cheddar cheeses before shaping into golf-ball-sized pieces.
5. Cook dough pieces in the parchment-lined air fryer for eight to ten minutes.

Bananarama Breakfast Bread

Nutritional Facts: Calories 180 Fat 6.0 g Protein 4.0 g Carbohydrates 29.0 g

Prep Time: 20 min Cook time: 15 min

Servings: 8

Ingredients:

- Cinnamon (1 teaspoon)
- Eggs, large, beaten lightly (2 pieces)
- Vanilla extract (1 teaspoon)
- Baking soda (1/4 teaspoon)
- Yogurt, nonfat, plain (1/3 cup)
- Walnuts, toasted, chopped coarsely (2 tablespoons)
- Flour, whole wheat, white (3/4 cup)
- Salt, kosher (1/2 teaspoon)
- Bananas, medium, ripe, mashed (2 pieces)
- Sugar, granulated (1/2 cup)
- Vegetable oil (2 tablespoons)
- Cooking spray

Directions:

1. Set the air fryer at 310 degrees Fahrenheit to preheat.
2. Mix the flour with baking soda, cinnamon, and salt.
3. Whisk the eggs together with the mashed bananas, yogurt, sugar, vanilla, and oil. Stir in the flour mixture to form your smooth batter.
4. Pour batter into a parchment-lined round cake pan (6-inch). Top with the walnuts and air-fry for thirty to thirty-five minutes.
5. Let cool before slicing. Serve right away.

Heartwarming Breakfast Buns

Nutritional Facts: Calories 230 Fat 0.5 g Protein 10.5 g Carbohydrates 46.0 g

Prep Time: 35 min Cook time: 25 min

Servings: 4

Ingredients:

- Baking powder (2 teaspoons)
- Greek yogurt, nonfat, plain (1 cup)
- Cinnamon (3/4 teaspoon)
- Egg white/whole egg, beaten (1 piece)
- Flour, all purpose, unbleached, whole wheat/gluten free (1 cup)
- Raw sugar (2 tablespoons)
- Kosher salt (1/2 teaspoon)
- Raisins (3 tablespoons)

Icing (reserve half):

- Water/milk (1 teaspoon)
- Powdered sugar (1/4 cup)

Directions:

1. Prepare the icing by whisking together the milk and powdered sugar. Pour the smooth mixture into a Ziploc bag.
2. Set the air fryer at 325 degrees Fahrenheit to preheat.
3. Cook the iced rolls in the air fryer for eleven to twelve minutes. Let cool.
4. Trim off the tip of the icing bag. Pipe the icing onto the rolls' surfaces in your desired pattern. (Reserve the remaining icing for another recipe.)

Breakfast Bagels

Nutritional Facts: Calories 152 Fat 0.3 g Protein 10.0 g Carbohydrates 26.5 g

Prep Time: 5 min Cook time: 25 min

Servings: 4

Ingredients:

- Baking powder (2 teaspoons)
- Flour, all purpose, whole wheat/gluten free, unbleached (1 cup)
- Greek yogurt, nonfat (1 cup)
- Kosher salt (3/4 teaspoon)
- Egg white, beaten (1 piece)

Toppings:

- Sesame seeds
- Dried garlic flakes
- Poppy seeds
- Dried onion flakes
- Other bagel seasonings

Directions:

1. Set the air fryer at 280 degrees Fahrenheit to preheat.
2. Whisk the flour, salt, and baking powder well. Stir in the yogurt to form a crumbly dough.
3. Turn out the dough onto a floured surface and knead until tacky. Shape into 4 balls, then roll each ball to form ¾-inch-thick cylinders that you join at the ends to make your bagels.
4. Brush bagels with egg wash before sprinkling with desired topping (not included in this recipe's calorie count). Place in the preheated air fryer and cook for fifteen minutes.

Filling Frittata

Nutritional Facts: Calories 233 Fat 15.0 g Protein 17.0 g Carbohydrates 6.0 g

Prep Time: 10 min Cook time: 15 min

Servings: 2

Ingredients:

- Milk (1/2 cup)
- Black pepper, freshly ground (1/2 teaspoon)
- Bell pepper, red, chopped (1/4 cup)
- Mushrooms, baby bella, chopped (1/4 cup)
- Salt (1/2 teaspoon)
- Eggs (4 pieces)
- Green onions, chopped (2 pieces)
- Spinach, chopped (1/4 cup)
- Cheddar cheese (1/4 cup)
- Hot sauce (1/4 teaspoon)

Directions:

1. Blend the milk and eggs by whisking well. Stir in the black pepper, salt, red bell pepper, hot sauce, green onions, cheddar cheese, spinach, and mushrooms.
2. Pour the egg mixture into a greased round pan (6x3-inch).
3. Cook in the sir fryer for fifteen to eighteen minutes at 360 degrees Fahrenheit.

Biscuit Bombs

Nutritional Facts: Calories 190 Fat 13.0 g Protein 7.0 g Carbohydrates 13.0 g

Prep Time: 30 min Cook time: 15 min

Servings: 10

Ingredients:

- Salt (1/8 teaspoon)
- Breakfast sausage, bulk (1/4 pound)
- Refrigerated biscuits, canned, flaky (10 1/5 ounces)
- Vegetable oil (1 tablespoon)
- Eggs, beaten (2 pieces)
- Pepper (1/8 teaspoon)
- Cheddar cheese, sharp, sliced into half-inch cubes (2 ounces)

Egg wash:

- Water (1 tablespoon)
- Egg (1 piece)

Directions:

1. Line the air fryer basket with parchment before coating with cooking spray.
2. Cook the sausage in oil until browned and crumbly. Set aside in a bowl.
3. In the same pan, stir the beaten eggs, pepper, and salt together and cook until moist and thickened. Add to the sausage bowl and mix well.
4. Separate the dough and press into 10 four-inch rounds. Fill each round with the egg mixture (1 tablespoon), then add a piece of cheese on top. Fold and pinch to seal before brushing with egg wash.
5. Add 5 biscuit bombs to the air fryer basket. Cover with another parchment paper coated with cooking spray, then place the remaining 5 biscuit bombs on top. Cook for eight minutes.

6. Remove the top parchment paper and arrange all biscuit bombs in a single layer. Air-fry for another four to six minutes.

Breakfast Biscuit Sliders

Nutritional Facts: Calories 130 Fat 6.0 g Protein 5.0 g Carbohydrates 14.0 g

Prep Time: 20 min Cook time: 35 min

Servings: 24

Ingredients:

- Ham, black forest, quartered (6 slices)
- Maple syrup, real (1 tablespoon)
- Swiss cheese, quartered (6 slices)
- Strawberry jam (1/2 cup)
- Refrigerated biscuits, canned, buttermilk (16 3/10 ounces)
- Deli turkey, quartered (6 slices)
- Butter, melted (1 tablespoon)
- Sugar, powdered (1 tablespoon)

Directions:

1. Set the air fryer at 325 degrees Fahrenheit to preheat.
2. Prep a 9x13-inch baking dish (3-quart) by misting with cooking spray.
3. Separate the dough to form eight biscuits. Slice each biscuit to form three strips. Press each strip to form 4 x 1.5-inch rectangle.
4. Fold all rectangles at the center, then fill half of each with one piece each of turkey, ham, and cheese. Cover with the unfilled side of the dough without sealing.
5. Arrange the filled biscuits in the baking dish and brush with a mixture of maple syrup and melted butter.
6. Cook in the air fryer for twenty-four minutes. Serve topped with powdered sugar, along with the strawberry jam.

Cheesecake Strawberry Cookies

Nutritional Facts: Calories 190 Fat 11.0 g Protein 2.0 g Carbohydrates 22.0 g

Prep Time: 20 min Cook time: 2 hrs 5 min

Servings: 24

Ingredients:

Base:

- Graham cracker crumbs (1/2 cup)
- Egg (1 piece)
- Sugar cookie mix (17.5 ounces)
- Butter, softened (3/4 cup)

Filling:

- Sugar (1/4 cup)
- Vanilla (1/4 teaspoon)
- Cream cheese, softened (8 ounces)
- Egg (1 piece)

Topping:

- Strawberries, fresh, chopped (1 cup)

Directions:

1. Set the air fryer at 325 degrees Fahrenheit to preheat.
2. Mist cooking spray onto 24 muffin cups.
3. Combine all base ingredients to form a soft dough. Shape into 24 rounds and place inside the muffin cups. Press a finger on top of each muffin to create a tiny indentation. Air-fry for ten minutes.

4. Beat the sugar and cream cheese together until smooth. Beat in the egg; once blended, beat in the vanilla. Add a tablespoon of this filling on top of each cooked cookie.

5. Air-fry for another eight minutes. Let cool before refrigerating for an hour.

6. Serve each cookie topped with a teaspoon of chopped strawberries.

Potato Quiche Minis

Nutritional Facts: Calories 90 Fat 6.0 g Protein 6.0 g Carbohydrates 2.0 g

Prep Time: 10 min Cook time: 30 min

Servings: 10

Ingredients:

- Swiss cheese, shredded (1/2 cup)
- Salt (1 teaspoon)
- Flour (1 tablespoon)
- Eggs (6 pieces)
- Baby spinach, packed (1 cup)
- Hash browns, refrigerated (2 cups)
- Sweet onion (1/4 piece)
- Olive oil, extra virgin (1 tablespoon)
- Milk (1/4 cup)
- Black pepper, freshly ground (1 teaspoon)

Directions:

1. Set the air fryer at 350 degrees Fahrenheit to preheat.
2. Coat a muffin tin (12 cups) with cooking spray.
3. Mix the flour and hash browns together. Form the crust by pressing the hash browns between ten muffin wells. Air-fry for twelve minutes.
4. Chop the spinach and onion into small chunks. Cook in olive oil. Once the spinach wilts, stir into a well-blended mixture of eggs, milk, pepper, salt, and cheese.
5. Pour the spinach-egg mixture inside the hash-browns-lined muffin wells and air-fry for another twelve minutes.

Sausage & Cheese Biscuit Cups

Nutritional Facts: Calories 220 Fat 14.0 g Protein 7.0 g Carbohydrates 18.0 g

Prep Time: 10 min Cook time: 25 min

Servings: 12

Ingredients:

- Breakfast sausage, cooked, cooled, crumbled (1 cup)

- Cheddar cheese, shredded (1 ½ cups)

- Buttermilk biscuits, canned, refrigerated (16 1/3 ounces)

Directions:

1. Set the air fryer at 325 degrees Fahrenheit to preheat.

2. Coat 12 muffin cups generously with cooking spray.

3. Combine the sausage with cheese.

4. Separate the dough so you have 8 biscuits. Cut each biscuit to form 6 pieces. Stir all biscuit pieces into the sausage and cheese mixture.

5. Fill each muffin cup with 3 biscuit pieces. Top each with any remaining sausage-cheese-mixture before covering with the rest of the biscuits.

6. Cook in the air fryer for eighteen minutes. Let cool before serving.

Mexican Style Hash Brown Cups

Nutritional Facts: Calories 140 Fat 6.0 g Protein 3.0 g Carbohydrates 18.0 g

Prep Time: 15 min Cook time: 1 hr 15 min

Servings: 12

Ingredients:

- Vegetable oil (2 tablespoons)
- Sour cream (1/4 cup)
- Green chiles, canned, drained, patted dry, chopped (4 ½ ounces)
- Cilantro leaves, fresh, chopped (1 tablespoon)
- Hash brown potatoes, bagged, shredded, refrigerated (20 ounces)
- Taco seasoning mix (2 tablespoons)
- Mexican cheese blend, shredded (1 cup)
- Green onion, sliced thinly (1 piece)

Directions:

1. Set the air fryer at 370 degrees Fahrenheit to preheat.
2. Mist cooking spray into 12 muffin cups.
3. Combine the potatoes with the taco seasoning and oil. Lightly press the potato mixture into the muffin cups.
4. Air-fry for forty-eight minutes. Top the muffins with green chiles and cheese, then air-fry for another four minutes.
5. Serve topped with sour cream, cilantro, and green onion.

Sugar Cinnamon Muffins

Nutritional Facts: Calories 306.6 Fat 10.4 g Protein 5.5 g Carbohydrates 48.4 g

Prep Time: 15 min Cook time: 20 min

Servings: 6

Ingredients:

- Butter (1/4 cup)
- Cinnamon (1 teaspoon)
- French bread, canned, refrigerated (11 ounces)
- Sugar (1/2 cup)
- Nutmeg (1/4 teaspoon)

Directions:

1. Set the air fryer at 325 degrees Fahrenheit to preheat.
2. Mist cooking spray into a muffin tin.
3. Brown the butter until nutty-smelling and caramelized but not burned.
4. Stir the sugar, nutmeg, and cinnamon together.
5. With a sharp knife and a cutting board, cut the French bread dough into discs.
6. Flatten discs with your rolling pin before brushing with melted butter and dipping in the sugar-cinnamon mixture.
7. Fill the prepped muffin tins with the remaining melted butter and sugar-cinnamon mixture.
8. Stack together 5 dough discs, then slice through in half and add to a muffin tin. Repeat with the rest of the dough discs.
9. Cook in the air fryer for sixteen minutes. Let cool before serving.

Apple Fritter Casserole

Nutritional Facts: Calories 290 Fat 14.0 g Protein 3.0 g Carbohydrates 37.0 g

Prep Time: 20 min Cook time: 55 min

Servings: 12

Ingredients:

- Butter, melted (3/4 cup)
- Brown sugar, packed (3/4 cup)
- Cinnamon, ground (1 teaspoon)
- Milk (2 teaspoons)
- Apple, granny smith, medium, peeled, cored, chopped (1 piece)
- Flour, all purpose (1 tablespoon)
- Crescent dinner rolls, canned, refrigerated (16 ounces)
- Sugar, powdered (1/2 cup)

Directions:

1. Set the oven at 325 degrees Fahrenheit to preheat.
2. Coat an 8x8-inch glass baking dish (2-quart) with cooking spray.
3. Stir together the apple, flour, cinnamon (1/2 teaspoon), and brown sugar (1/2 cup).
4. Sprinkle cinnamon (1/2 teaspoon) and brown sugar (4 tablespoons) over unrolled dough, pressing them lightly to stick. Cut the dough to form one-inch squares, then mix with the apples.
5. Transfer the dough-apple mixture into the baking dish. Cover with melted butter before cooking in the air fryer for thirty-two minutes.
6. Let cool before drizzling with a mixture of milk and powdered sugar. Serve right away.

French Toast Cups

Nutritional Facts: Calories 380 Fat 20.0 g Protein 5.0 g Carbohydrates 45.0 g

Prep Time: 10 min Cook time: 20 min

Servings: 6

Ingredients:

- Sugar (1/3 cup)
- Egg, whole (1 piece)
- Biscuit mix, plain (2 cups)
- Milk (2/3 cup)
- Oil (2 tablespoons)

Topping:

- Cinnamon (1/2 teaspoon)
- Sugar (1/4 cup)
- Butter, melted (1/4 cup)

Directions:

1. Set the air fryer at 370 degrees Fahrenheit to preheat.
2. Mist cooking spray onto a muffin tin.
3. Combine the biscuit mix with egg, milk, oil, and sugar. Pour into the muffin tin.
4. Cook in the air fryer for twelve minutes. Let cool.
5. Dip the muffins in melted butter before coating with a mixture of sugar and cinnamon.

Cinnamon Roll Cupcakes

Nutritional Facts: Calories 80 Fat 2.0 g Protein 1.0 g Carbohydrates 14.0 g

Prep Time: 5 min Cook time: 15 min

Servings: 20

Ingredients:

- Cinnamon rolls, w/ icing pack included, canned, refrigerated (17 ½ ounces)
- Sprinkles (1 tablespoon)

Directions:

1. Set the air fryer at 325 degrees Fahrenheit to preheat.
2. Use mini cupcake wrappers to line mini muffin tin (24 cups).
3. Slice the cinnamon rolls to form 24 pieces.
4. Press each piece into a muffin cup.
5. Air-fry for eight minutes. Let cool before drizzling with icing.
6. Serve topped with sprinkles.

Peanut Butter Breakfast Muffins

Nutritional Facts: Calories 180 Fat 9.0 g Protein 5.0 g Carbohydrates 19.0 g

Prep Time: 10 min Cook time: 15 min

Servings: 12

Ingredients:

- Milk (2/3 cup)
- Maple syrup (1/4 cup)
- Biscuit mix, plain (2 cups)
- Egg (1 piece)
- Peanut butter, creamy (1/2 cup)
- Maple syrup (1 teaspoon)
- Chocolate chips (1/4 cup)

Directions:

1. Set the air fryer at 325 degrees Fahrenheit to preheat.
2. Line your cupcake pan with cupcake liners.
3. Mix the biscuit mix with milk, peanut butter, eggs, and syrup.
4. Fill each cupcake tin with the batter and top with chocolate chips.
5. Cook in the air fryer for twelve minutes.
6. Serve drizzled with extra maple syrup.

Easy Irish Soda Breakfast Bread

Nutritional Facts: Calories 110 Fat 3.0 g Protein 3.0 g Carbohydrates 19.0 g

Prep Time: 10 min Cook time: 30 min

Servings: 1

Ingredients:

- Flour, all purpose (2 ½ cups)
- Salt (1/2 teaspoon)
- Baking soda (1 teaspoon)
- Buttermilk (3/4 cup)
- Butter, softened (3 tablespoons)
- Sugar (2 tablespoons)
- Baking powder (1 teaspoon)
- Raisins (1/3 cup)

Directions:

1. Set the air fryer at 350 degrees Fahrenheit to preheat.
2. Coat a cookie sheet with a little oil or butter.
3. Use a pastry blender to mix the butter into a mixture of flour, baking powder, sugar, salt, and baking powder. Stir the raisins and buttermilk into the crumbly mixture to form a tacky dough.
4. Knead the dough on a floured surface until smooth. Mold into a 6.5-inch round loaf. Use a floured knife to cut an "X" half-an-inch-deep into the loaf.
5. Air-fry for thirty minutes. If preferred, serve brushed with softened margarine.

Migas Muffins

Nutritional Facts: Calories 210 Fat 15.0 g Protein 10.0 g Carbohydrates 7.0 g

Prep Time: 15 min Cook time: 20 min

Servings: 6

Ingredients:

- Vegetable oil (2 tablespoons)
- Eggs, large, scrambled (6 pieces)
- Red onion, diced (1/4 cup)
- Pepper (1/4 teaspoon)
- Salt (1/4 teaspoon)
- Corn tortillas, small, sliced (3 pieces)
- Bell pepper, red, diced (1/2 piece)
- Serrano pepper, small, seeded, minced (1 piece)
- Cheddar cheese, grated (3 ounces)

Directions:

1. Set the air fryer at 305 degrees Fahrenheit to preheat.
2. Cook the sliced corn strips in oil (1 tablespoon) until light brown and crisp. Set aside.
3. Cook the onions, Serrano, and peppers in a little oil until softened. Season with pepper and salt.
4. Grease 6 muffin tins with a little oil before filling with the corn strips. Top with the pepper mixture as well as grated cheese. Finish by adding equal portions of scrambled eggs.
5. Air-fry for twenty minutes. Let sit for five minutes before serving.

Bacon Cupcakes

Nutritional Facts: Calories 190 Fat 9.0 g Protein 8.0 g Carbohydrates 17.0 g

Prep Time: 15 min Cook time: 45 min

Servings: 12

Ingredients:

- Bacon, crisply cooked, crumbled (3/4 cup)
- Vegetable oil (2 tablespoons)
- Milk (2 tablespoons)
- Pepper (1/4 teaspoon)
- Cheddar cheese shredded (3/4 cup)
- Hash brown potatoes, shredded, refrigerated (20 ounces)
- Salt (1/2 teaspoon)
- Eggs (6 pieces)
- Sriracha sauce

Directions:

1. Set the air fryer at 370 degrees Fahrenheit to preheat.
2. Line 12 muffin cups with foil liners misted with cooking spray.
3. Combine the potatoes, pepper, oil, and salt before pressing into the muffin cups. Air-fry for thirty-five minutes.
4. Beat the eggs along with milk, then mix with the cheese and bacon. Press down the cooked potatoes in their muffin cups before topping each with the egg mixture (1/4 cup).
5. Return the muffin cups to the air fryer and cook for ten minutes. Let cool before serving with sauce.

Wake-Me-Up Focaccia

Nutritional Facts: Calories 200 Fat 3.0 g Protein 4.0 g Carbohydrates 39.0 g

Prep Time: 10 min Cook time: 20 min

Servings: 6

Ingredients:

- French bread, refrigerated (11 ounces)
- Apricot preserves (3 tablespoons)
- Pecans, chopped (1 tablespoon)

Directions:

1. Set the air fryer at 325 degrees Fahrenheit to preheat.
2. Press the dough into an 8-inch circle. Once evenly thick and free of bubbles, sprinkle with pecans.
3. Cook in the air fryer for twenty minutes.
4. Heat the preserves in the microwave until softened. Spread on top of the hot focaccia.
5. Serve sliced into wedges.

Easy Pancake Cups

Nutritional Facts: Calories 80 Fat 4.5 g Protein 3.0 g Carbohydrates 6.0 g

Prep Time: 5 min *Cook time:* 15 min

Servings: 18

Ingredients:

- Eggs (6 pieces)
- Salt (1/2 teaspoon)
- Butter (1/4 cup)
- Milk (1 cup)
- Flour (1 cup)
- Vanilla (1 teaspoon)

Toppings:

- Scramble eggs
- Cooked sausage
- Jam/preserves

Directions:

1. Set the air fryer at 370 degrees Fahrenheit to preheat.
2. Process the eggs, milk, flour, vanilla, and salt in the blender to combine. Add ½ of butter and process; repeat.
3. Grease 18 muffin cups by misting with cooking spray. Pour batter (1/4 cup) into each cup.
4. Cook in the air fryer for fifteen minutes.
5. Let pancake cups sit for two minutes before topping with desired toppings.

Mexican Breakfast Dish

Nutritional Facts: Calories 300 Fat 15.0 g Protein 17.0 g Carbohydrates 23.0 g

Prep Time: 8 min Cook time: 25 min

Servings: 6

Ingredients:

- Bell pepper, green, diced (1/3 cup)
- Green chile, fire roasted, fresh/canned (2 tablespoons)
- Cumin, ground (1/2 teaspoon)
- Cheddar cheese, shredded (1 ½ cups)
- Black beans, drained, rinsed (1 cup)
- Salt (1/2 teaspoon)
- Cilantro, fresh, chopped (2 tablespoons)
- Potatoes, packaged, country style (1 ¼ cups)
- Bell pepper, red, diced (1/3 cup)
- Corn, frozen, thawed (1/2 cup)
- Eggs, large (6 pieces)
- Black pepper (1/4 teaspoon)
- Green onions, chopped (1/4 cup)
- Salsa
- Sour cream
- Olive oil

Directions:

1. Set the air fryer at 350 degrees Fahrenheit to preheat.
2. Use a little olive oil to grease a glass pan (9x9).
3. Sauté potato in olive oil (2 teaspoons) for two minutes. Stir in bell peppers and cook for another three minutes. Turn off heat and stir in corn, green chile, and beans.

4. Whisk the eggs together with the pepper, cumin, and salt. Mix with the cheese (1 cup), cilantro, and green onion. Pour into the veggie mixture and combine.

5. Fill the prepped pan with the mixture and top with the remaining cheese (1/2 cup). Cook in the air fryer for twenty-five minutes.

6. Let sit for five minutes before slicing into squares and serving with sour cream or salsa.

Baklavas for Breakfast

Nutritional Facts: Calories 340 Fat 11.0 g Protein 6.0 g Carbohydrates 53.0 g

Prep Time: 35 min Cook time: 15 min

Servings: 8

Ingredients:

Biscuits:

- Butter biscuits, flaky layers, refrigerated (16 1/3 ounces)

Filling:

- Walnut halves/pieces (1/4 cup)
- Cinnamon, ground (1/2 teaspoon)
- Almonds, sliced, blanched (1/2 cup)
- Sugar (1 tablespoon)
- Salt (1/4 teaspoon)

Syrup:

- Lemon juice (2 teaspoons)
- Honey (1/2 cup)
- Sugar (1/4 cup)
- Water (1/3 cup)
- Cinnamon, ground (1/8 teaspoon)
- Cloves, whole (3 pieces)
- Salt (1/4 teaspoon)

Directions:

1. Set the air fryer at 325 degrees Fahrenheit to preheat.
2. Prep 8 muffin cups by spraying with cooking spray.

3. Combine the syrup ingredients before heating to boiling point. Let cool, then remove the cloves.

4. Blend the filling ingredients in the food processor.

5. Separate the dough to form 8 biscuits, then separate each to form three layers.

6. Line a muffin cup with one biscuit layer; brush with syrup before topping with nut filling (1 ½ teaspoons) and drizzling with syrup (1 ½ teaspoons). Repeat the process twice.

7. Repeat step 6 until all biscuits, nut filling, and syrup (reserve the remaining ½ cup) are used up.

8. Cook in the air fryer for fifteen minutes. Let sit in the muffin pan for one minute before serving with the reserved syrup.

Cheesy Sausage and Egg Rolls

Nutritional Facts: Calories 270 Fat 20.0g Protein 10.0 g Carbohydrates 13.0 g

Prep Time: 15 min Cook time: 15 min

Servings: 8

Ingredients:

- Cheddar cheese slices, sandwich size (4 pieces)
- Crescent rolls, refrigerated (8 ounces)
- Eggs (3 pieces)
- Breakfast sausage links, fully cooked (8 pieces)
- Salt (1/4 teaspoon)
- Pepper (1/4 teaspoon)

Directions:

1. Set the air fryer at 325 degrees Fahrenheit to preheat.
2. Beat the eggs; reserve one tablespoon as egg wash and scramble the rest.
3. Halve the cheese slices.
4. Separate the dough into 8 triangles. Top each triangle with a half-slice of cheese, a tablespoon of scrambled eggs, and a sausage link. Loosely roll up all filled triangles before placing in the air fryer basket. Brush with the reserved egg wash and sprinkle all over with pepper and salt.
5. Cook for fifteen minutes.
6. Serve right away.

Oatmeal Yogurt Bars

Nutritional Facts: Calories 330 Fat 15.0 g Protein 7.0 g Carbohydrates 43.0 g

Prep Time: 15 min Cook time: 25 min

Servings: 8

Ingredients:

Oatmeal layer:

- Milk (1/4 cup)
- Flour, whole wheat, white (1 cup)
- Brown sugar (1/2 cup)
- Salt (1/2 teaspoon)
- Butter, melted (1/2 cup)
- Oats, old fashioned, rolled (1 ½ cups)
- Baking soda (1/2 teaspoon)
- Cinnamon (1/2 teaspoon)
- Egg (1 piece)

Yogurt layer:

- Yogurt, strawberry-flavored (3/4 cup)
- Flour, whole wheat, white (2 tablespoons)
- Strawberries, frozen, thawed, chopped (1 cup)
- Egg (1 piece)

Directions:

1. Set the air fryer at 325 degrees Fahrenheit to preheat.
2. Use parchment paper to line a square baking dish (8x8-inch).
3. Stir the oats and flour together with cinnamon, baking soda, sugar, and salt.
4. Whisk the egg together with milk and melted butter.

5. Stir the liquid mixture into the dry mixture. Reserve half a cup of the resulting oat mixture; pour the rest into the baking dish, pressing so it form a solid crust.

6. Stir the yogurt layer ingredients together. Spread on top of the oat mixture crust to form an even layer.

7. Cook in the air fryer for twenty-five minutes. Let cool before slicing into 8 bars.

Cinnamon Roll Cupcake Minis

Nutritional Facts: Calories 80 Fat 2.0 g Protein 1.0 g Carbohydrates 14.0 g

Prep Time: 5 min Cook time: 10 min

Servings: 20

Ingredients:

- Cinnamon rolls, w/ icing, refrigerated (17 ½ ounces)
- Sprinkles (1 tablespoon)

Directions:

1. Set the air fryer at 325 degrees Fahrenheit to preheat.
2. Use cupcake wrappers to line a mini muffin tin (24 cups).
3. After setting aside the icing pack, slice each of the cinnamon rolls to form 4 pieces. Shape into mini rolls and press into the lined tins.
4. Cook in the air fryer for ten minutes. Serve drizzled with icing and topped with sprinkles.

Mexican Style Egg Bake

Nutritional Facts: Calories 280 Fat 16.0 g Protein 21.0 g Carbohydrates 15.0 g

Prep Time: 20 min Cook time: 50 min

Servings: 12

Ingredients:

- Pepper, ground (1/4 teaspoon)
- Taco seasoning mix (1 ounce)
- Cheddar cheese, shredded (2 cups)
- Onion, chopped (1/2 cup)
- Salt (1/2 teaspoon)
- Hash brown potatoes, shredded, cooked, refrigerated (20 ounces)
- Turkey breakfast sausage, bulk (1 pound)
- Eggs (12 pieces)
- Milk (1/4 cup)
- Salsa, chunky, thick (1 ½ cups)

Directions:

1. Preheat the air fryer to 325 degrees Fahrenheit.
2. Prep a 2x9x13-inch baking dish (3-quart) with cooking spray.
3. Toss the hash brown potatoes together with taco seasoning mix (1 tablespoon). Place in the baking dish.
4. Mist cooking spray onto a skillet (10-inch) before heating on medium-high. Add the onion and sausage and cook for five to seven minutes. Drain and set aside.
5. Whisk the rest of your taco seasoning mix with the eggs, milk, pepper, salt, and cheese. Stir in the salsa and sausage mixture before pouring on top of the hash browns.
6. Air-fry for forty minutes.
7. Serve after letting stand for ten minutes.

So Good! Peanut Butter Muffins

Nutritional Facts: Calories 230 Fat 11.0 g Protein 6.0 g Carbohydrates 27.0 g

Prep Time: 15 min Cook time: 30 min

Servings: 12

Ingredients:

- Flour, whole wheat (1/2 cup)
- Milk (1 cup)
- Vegetable oil (2 tablespoons)
- Sugar, light brown, packed (1/3 cup)
- Banana, large, ripe, mashed (1 piece)
- Chia seeds (1 tablespoon)
- Flour, all purpose, unbleached (1/2 cup)
- Granola bars, crunchy, peanut butter, ground (3/4 cup)
- Baking powder (1 tablespoon)
- Peanut butter, creamy (1/2 cup)
- Egg (1 piece)
- Vanilla (1 teaspoon)

Directions:

1. Preheat the air fryer at 325 degrees Fahrenheit.
2. Use baking paper cups to line a muffin tin (12 cups).
3. Whisk the ground granola bars along with the baking powder, flours, and brown sugar.
4. In a separate bowl, whisk the mashed banana along with the peanut butter, egg, milk, vanilla, and vegetable oil.
5. Stir the chia seeds and wet mixture together with the dry mixture.
6. Pour your batter into the muffin cups and air-fry for twenty to twenty-five minutes.
7. Let cool, then serve.

Strawberry Chia Muffins

Nutritional Facts: Calories 140 Fat 2.5 g Protein 3.0 g Carbohydrates 26.0 g

Prep Time: 10 min Cook time: 20 min

Servings: 12

Ingredients:

- Greek yogurt, vanilla (1/3 cup)
- Water (3/4 cup)
- Strawberries, chopped (2/3 cup)
- Muffin mix, w/ blueberries included (1 box)
- Eggs (2 pieces)
- Chia seeds (3 tablespoons)

Directions:

1. Preheat the air fryer at 325 degrees Fahrenheit.
2. Line your cupcake pan with baking paper.
3. Blend the muffin mix together with eggs, yogurt, chia seeds, and water.
4. Rinse the blueberries included in your muffin mix, then drain and add to the batter. Fold, along with the strawberries, into the batter.
5. Pour batter into the lined cups and air-fry for twenty minutes.

Cheesy Broccoli Muffins

Nutritional Facts: Calories 140 Fat 9.0 g Protein 4.0 g Carbohydrates 11.0 g

Prep Time: 12 min Cook time: 33 min

Servings: 12

Ingredients:

- Egg, large (1 piece)
- Milk, whole (1/2 cup)
- Cheddar cheese, sharp, shredded (1 cup)
- Biscuit mix (1 ½ cups)
- Vegetable oil (3 tablespoons)
- Broccoli cuts, frozen, steamed until tender-crisp, drained, chopped finely (1/2 cup)
- Onion powder (1/4 teaspoon)

Directions:

1. Preheat the air fryer at 375 degrees Fahrenheit.
2. Mist cooking spray into a muffin pan (12-cup).
3. Combine the biscuit mix, egg, milk, and oil together.
4. Stir in the onion powder, cheese, and broccoli.
5. Fill the muffin cups with the batter.
6. Cook in the air fryer for ten minutes.
7. Serve after letting cool for five minutes.

Honey Blueberry Breakfast Muffins

Nutritional Facts: Calories 170 Fat 5.0 g Protein 3.0 g Carbohydrates 27.0 g

Prep Time: 15 min Cook time: 20 min

Servings: 12

Ingredients:

- Salt (1/2 teaspoon)
- Cinnamon, ground (1/4 teaspoon)
- Egg (1 piece)
- Baking powder (3 teaspoons)
- Vegetable oil (1/4 cup)
- Flour, whole wheat (1 cup)
- Brown sugar, packed (2 tablespoons)
- Milk, fat free (3/4 cup)
- Honey (1/4 cup)
- Flour, all purpose (1 cup)
- Blueberries, frozen (1 cup)

Directions:

1. Set the air fryer at 375 degrees Fahrenheit to preheat.
2. Stir the cinnamon and sugar together.
3. Beat the egg along with the milk, honey, and oil. Stir in the baking powder, flours, and salt. Fold the blueberries into the lumpy batter.
4. Pour batter into 12 lined muffin cups and top with the sugar-cinnamon mixture. Air-fry for twenty minutes.

Hot Caramel Muffins

Nutritional Facts: Calories 430 Fat 16.0 g Protein 5.0 g Carbohydrates 68.0 g

Prep Time: 15 min *Cook time:* 15 min

Servings: 6

Ingredients:

- Cinnamon, ground (1 ½ teaspoons)
- Butter (1/4 cup)
- Water (2 teaspoons)
- Sugar, granulated (1/4 cup)
- Biscuits, refrigerated, flaky layers (16 1/3 ounces)
- Brown sugar, packed (2/3 cup)

Directions:

1. Preheat the air fryer at 350 degrees Fahrenheit.
2. Prep 6 muffin cups by misting with cooking spray.
3. Separate and cut the dough so you end up with 6 biscuit pieces from each biscuit. Roll in a mixture of cinnamon and granulated sugar.
4. Fill each muffin cup with 8 of the biscuit pieces.
5. Dissolve the brown sugar in water and butter by stirring the ingredients for two minutes over medium heat. Set aside 2 tablespoons of the resulting caramel mixture and drizzle the rest over the filled muffin cups.
6. Air-fry for eight to eleven minutes. Drizzle with caramel and serve.

Cinnamon Overload Muffins

Nutritional Facts: Calories 220 Fat 10.0 g Protein 3.0 g Carbohydrates 29.0 g

Prep Time: 15 min Cook time: 20 min

Servings: 12

Ingredients:

Muffins:

- Sugar (1/2 cup)
- Milk (2/3 cup)
- Egg (1 piece)
- Flour, self-rising (2 cups)
- Cinnamon, ground (1/4 teaspoon)
- Butter, melted, cooled (1/3 cup)

Topping:

- Cinnamon, ground (1 teaspoon)
- Sugar (1/4 cup)
- Butter, melted (1/4 cup)

Directions:

1. Preheat the air fryer at 400 degrees Fahrenheit.
2. Prep 12 muffin cups with cooking spray or paper liners.
3. Mix the flour together with sugar (1/2 cup) and cinnamon (1/4 teaspoon).
4. Blend the egg, milk, and melted butter (1/3 cup) together, then stir into the flour mixture.
5. Pour into the muffin cups and air-fry for fifteen to eighteen minutes.
6. Dip each warm muffin into melted butter (1/4 cup) before dipping into a mixture of cinnamon (1 teaspoon) and sugar (1/4 cup).
7. Serve and enjoy.

Mocha Goodness Muffins

Nutritional Facts: Calories 250 Fat 11.0 g Protein 4.0 g Carbohydrates 33.0 g

Prep Time: 10 min Cook time: 20 min

Servings: 12

Ingredients:

- Egg (1 piece)
- Baking cocoa, unsweetened (2 tablespoons)
- Milk (1 cup)
- Salt (1/2 teaspoon)
- Coffee granules, instant (1 tablespoon)
- Flour, all purpose (2 cups)
- Baking powder (2 ½ teaspoons)
- Brown sugar, packed (1/3 cup)
- Vegetable oil (1/3 cup)
- Chocolate chips, semi-sweet (1 cup)

Directions:

1. Preheat the air fryer at 400 degrees Fahrenheit.
2. Use baking paper to line 12 muffin cups.
3. Combine the flour with salt, baking powder, and cocoa.
4. Beat the egg along with milk, coffee, brown sugar, and oil.
5. Add to the flour mixture and stir to combine.
6. Add the chocolate chunks and gently fold in.
7. Fill each muffin cup with the batter.
8. Cook in the air fryer for eighteen to twenty minutes.

Cranberry Apricot Breakfast Cups

Nutritional Facts: Calories 140 Fat 2.5 Protein 3.0 g Carbohydrates 26.0 g

Prep Time: 10 min Cook time: 20 min

Servings: 12

Ingredients:

- Milk (3/4 cup)
- Sugar (1/2 cup)
- Nutmeg, ground (1/2 teaspoon)
- Cranberries, dried (1/3 cup)
- Egg whites (2 pieces)
- Biscuit mix (1 ¾ cups)
- Apricots, dried, chopped (1/3 cup)
- Butter, melted (1 tablespoon)
- Cinnamon, ground (1/2 teaspoon)

Directions:

1. Preheat the air fryer at 325 degrees Fahrenheit.
2. Prep 12 muffin cups using paper cup liners.
3. Mix all ingredients. Add the batter to the muffin cups.
4. Air-fry for thirteen to eighteen minutes.

Sundried Tomato Muffins

Nutritional Facts: Calories 170 Fat 6.0 g Protein 7.0 g Carbohydrates 21.0 g

Prep Time: 15 min Cook time: 45 min

Servings: 12

Ingredients:

- Tomatoes, sundried, julienned (1/2 cup)
- Baking powder (2 teaspoons)
- Olive oil (2 tablespoons + 1 teaspoon)
- Baking soda (1/2 teaspoon)
- Mozzarella, fresh, cubed (4 ounces)
- Flour, all purpose (2 ¼ cups)
- Salt (1 ¼ teaspoons)
- Buttermilk (1 ¼ cups)
- Eggs (2 pieces)
- Basil, fresh, chopped (2 tablespoons)

Directions:

1. Preheat the air fryer at 325 degrees Fahrenheit. Meanwhile, mist cooking spray onto a muffin tin (12 cups).
2. Whisk the flour together with baking powder, baking soda, and salt.
3. Whisk the eggs together with the olive oil and buttermilk.
4. Stir the flour mixture and egg mixture together. Fold the sundried tomatoes, cubed mozzarella, and basil into the batter.
5. Pour the batter into the muffin cups. Cook in the air fryer for twenty to twenty-five minutes.
6. Serve warm.

Easy Savory Stuffing Breakfast Cupcakes

Nutritional Facts: Calories 190 Fat 10.0 g Protein 5.0 g Carbohydrates 20.0 g

Prep Time: 30 min Cook time: 60 min

Servings: 12

Ingredients:

- Sea salt (1/2 teaspoon)
- Walnuts, chopped (3/4 cup)
- Eggs, beaten (2 pieces)
- Thyme, dried (2 teaspoons)
- Apple, medium, pared, cored, cubed (1 piece)
- Sage, dried (1 teaspoon)
- Bread, Italian/French (1 pound)
- Butter (8 tablespoons)
- Celery ribs, chopped (3 pieces)
- Broth, chicken/vegetable, low sodium (1 ½ cups)
- Pepper

Directions:

1. Set the air fryer at 325 degrees Fahrenheit to preheat.
2. Slice the bread to form one-inch cubes.
3. Line a baking tray with parchment. Add the bread cubes. Air-fry for ten minutes.
4. Add the walnuts to the bread cubes and air-fry for another seven to eight minutes. Let everything cool for about ten minutes.
5. Stir the celery and apples into melted butter. Cook over medium heat for ten minutes. Set aside to cool.
6. Mix the bread cubes with the apple-celery mixture as well as the broth, eggs, pepper, salt, sage, and thyme.

7. Fill a paper-lined cupcake tray with the stuffing. Air-fry for thirty to thirty-five minutes.

Apple Streusel Bread

Nutritional Facts: Calories 310 Fat 9.0 g Protein 4.0 g Carbohydrates 54.0 g

Prep Time: 10 min Cook time: 50 min

Servings: 8

Ingredients:

- Milk (2 tablespoons)
- Brown sugar (1/4 cup)
- Applesauce, chunky (1 cup)
- Flour (1/4 cup)
- Cinnamon, ground (1 tablespoon)
- Sugar, powdered (1 tablespoon)
- Biscuits, refrigerated, flaky layers (16 1/3 ounces)
- Sugar (1/4 cup)
- Butter, melted, divided (2 tablespoons)
- Vanilla (1/2 teaspoon)

Directions:

1. Preheat the air fryer at 325 degrees Fahrenheit.
2. Mist cooking spray onto a loaf pan (9x5-inch) before lining with parchment.
3. Combine the applesauce with cinnamon and sugar.
4. Separate the dough into 16 biscuit rounds. Add a spoonful of the apple mixture onto each of 8 biscuit rounds. Cover all filled rounds with the remaining biscuit pieces.
5. Arrange the biscuit layers at the bottom of the loaf pan and cover with a mixture of flour, butter, and brown sugar. Air-fry for thirty-five to forty minutes.
6. Combine vanilla, milk, and sugar, then drizzle on top of your loaf before serving.

Jalapeno Bread Bake

Nutritional Facts: Calories 240 Fat 16.0 g Protein 9.0 g Carbohydrates 16.0 g

Prep Time: 10 min Cook time: 20 min

Servings: 10

Ingredients:

- Cream cheese block, softened (8 ounces)
- Cheddar, sharp, shredded (2 cups)
- French bread, refrigerated, baked following package directions (11 ounces)
- Onion salt (1 teaspoon)
- Jalapeno pepper, sliced finely (2 pieces)

Directions:

1. Preheat the air fryer at 375 degrees Fahrenheit.
2. Slice the baked French bread into lengthwise halves.
3. Beat the cream cheese along with the cheddar cheese (1/2 portion) and onion salt.
4. Coat the cut sides of your French bread halves with the cream cheese mixture before sprinkling with remaining cheddar and sliced jalapenos.
5. Air-fry for sixteen to twenty-one minutes. Let cool for five minutes, then slice into two-inch portions.
6. Enjoy.

Walnut Carrot Bread

Nutritional Facts: Calories 210 Fat 7.0 g Protein 4.0 g Carbohydrates 32.0 g

Prep Time: 15 min Cook time: 2 hrs 25 min

Servings: 16

Ingredients:

- Walnuts, chopped (1/2 cup)
- Carrots, canned, sliced, drained (14 ½ ounces)—reserve ½ cup of liquid
- Eggs (2 pieces)
- Pumpkin pie spice (2 teaspoons)
- Lemon juice (1/3 cup)
- Sugar (3/4 cup)
- Salt (1/4 teaspoon)
- Bran cereal (1 ½ cups)
- Lemon peel, grated (1 teaspoon)
- Vegetable oil (1/4 cup)
- Flour, all purpose (2 2/3 cups)
- Baking powder (2 teaspoons)
- Baking soda (1/2 teaspoon)

Directions:

1. Preheat the air fryer at 325 degrees Fahrenheit.
2. Use cooking spray to grease a loaf pan (9x5-inch).
3. Crush the cereal in the food processor.
4. Mash the carrots, before blending with reserved carrot liquid, lemon juice, eggs, oil, and lemon peel.
5. Add flour, baking powder, baking soda, sugar, salt, and pumpkin pie spice to the carrot mixture and beat until blended. Mix walnuts and crushed cereal into the batter.

6. Pour batter into the loaf pan and air-fry for one hour and ten minutes. Let cool, slice, and serve.

No-Fuss Cranberry Cobbler

Nutritional Facts: Calories 255 Fat 9.0 g Protein 0.5 g Carbohydrates 41.0 g

Prep Time: 5 min Cook time: 45 min

Servings: 16

Ingredients:

- Cranberry sauce, whole berry (28 ounces)
- Butter, melted (3/4 cup)
- Yellow cake mix, super moist (15 ¼ ounces)

Directions:

1. Preheat the air fryer at 325 degrees Fahrenheit.
2. Grease a baking dish (9x13-inch) using cooking spray. Fill with cranberry sauce, spreading to form an even layer. Top with dry cake mix, then cover with melted butter.
3. Cook in the air fryer for forty-five to fifty minutes.
4. Let cool for fifteen minutes. Serve in individual bowls.

Tuna Breakfast Casserole

Nutritional Facts: Calories 320 Fat 11.0 g Protein 28.0 g Carbohydrates 31.0 g

Prep Time: 15 min Cook time: 25 min

Servings: 4

Ingredients:

- Water, cold (1/3 cup)
- Tuna, canned, drained (10 ounces)
- Sweet pickle relish (2 tablespoons)
- Milk (1/2 cup)
- Biscuit mix (1 cup)
- Mixed vegetables, frozen (1 ½ cups)
- Soup, cream of chicken, condensed (10 ¾ ounces)
- Pimientos, sliced, drained (2 ounces)
- Lemon juice (1 teaspoon)
- Paprika

Directions:

1. Preheat the air fryer at 375 degrees Fahrenheit.
2. Grease a round casserole (1 ½ quarts) using cooking spray.
3. Mix the frozen vegetables with milk, tuna, relish, soup, lemon juice, and pimientos. Stir over medium heat for six to eight minutes, then pour into the greased casserole.
4. Combine the biscuit mix with cold water to form a soft dough. Take 4 spoons of the dough and drop into the tuna mixture; repeat until all the dough is used up.
5. Air-fry for twenty to twenty-five minutes.

Apple Cookie Cobbler

Nutritional Facts: Calories 290 Fat 8.0 g Protein 1.5 g Carbohydrates 52.5 g

Prep Time: 15 min Cook time: 45 min

Servings: 12

Ingredients:

- Brown sugar, packed (1 cup)
- Lemon juice (2 tablespoons)
- Cinnamon, ground (1 ½ teaspoons)
- Sugar, granulated (2 tablespoons)
- Apples, peeled, sliced (6 cups)
- Flour, all purpose (2 tablespoons)
- Allspice, ground (1/2 teaspoon)
- Sugar cookies, refrigerated (1 roll)

Directions:

1. Preheat the air fryer at 325 degrees Fahrenheit.
2. Combine the apples with flour, brown sugar, cinnamon (1 teaspoon), lemon juice, and allspice.
3. Add apple mixture to a glass pie plate (9.5-inch deep-dish). Top with the cookie dough, spreading to form an even layer. Sprinkle all over with a mixture of cinnamon (1/2 teaspoon) and granulated sugar.
4. Air-fry for thirty-five to forty-five minutes.

Apple Muffin Bake

Nutritional Facts: Calories 400 Fat 10.0 g Protein 4.0 g Carbohydrates 73.0 g

Prep Time: 15 min Cook time: 25 min

Servings: 6

Ingredients:

Filling:

- Dark rum (1/4 cup)
- Apples, firm, large, peeled, cored, sliced (5 pieces)
- Nutmeg, ground (1/2 teaspoon)
- Butter (2 tablespoons)
- Sugar, light brown, packed (3/4 cup)
- Cinnamon, ground (1/2 teaspoon)
- Ginger, ground (1/4 teaspoon)

Topping:

- Milk (1/3 cup)
- Egg (1 piece)
- Cornbread/muffin mix (1 pouch)
- Butter, melted (2 tablespoons)

Directions:

1. Preheat the air fryer at 350 degrees Fahrenheit.
2. Use cooking spray to grease a glass-baking dish (8-inch square).
3. Melt butter (2 tablespoons). Stir in the rest of the filling ingredients and cook for five minutes.
4. Pour filling into the baking dish, then cover completely with a mixture of cornbread topping ingredients.
5. Air-fry for twenty to twenty-five minutes.

Raspberry Peach Cobbler

Nutritional Facts: Calories 15 Fat 13.0 g Protein 4.0 g Carbohydrates 72.0 g

Prep Time: 40 min Cook time: 1 hr 20 min

Servings: 8

Ingredients:

- Butter, cold (1/3 cup)
- Cornstarch (6 tablespoons)
- Raspberries, fresh (2 cups)
- Peaches, fresh/frozen, peeled, sliced (8 cups)
- Vanilla (2 teaspoons)
- Sugar (1 1/3 cups + 2 tablespoons)
- Flour, all purpose (1 cup)
- Ice water (3 tablespoons)
- Cinnamon, ground (1/2 teaspoon)
- Butter (3 tablespoons)
- Egg, slightly beaten (1 piece)

Directions:

1. Cut the butter into the flour to form a crumbly mixture. Moisten the mixture with water, added tablespoon by tablespoon. Flatten the moist pastry into a ball, wrap in cling film, and chill for one hour.
2. Grease 4 ramekins (10-ounce) with butter before placing on a cookie sheet.
3. Combine the peaches with sugar (1 1/3 cups), cinnamon, vanilla, and cornstarch before heating on medium and cooking for five minutes. Stir in butter (3 tablespoons), then the raspberries.
4. Fill the ramekins with the raspberry peach mixture.

5. Cut the chilled pastry into 5x3/4-inch strips and lay on top of the ramekins to form crisscross patterns. Brush with egg before sprinkling with sugar (2 tablespoons).

6. Cook in the air fryer for twenty minutes.

Turkey Meatloaf Muffins

Nutritional Facts: Calories 360 Fat 20.0 g Protein 29.0 g Carbohydrates 13.0 g

Prep Time: 20 min Cook time: 25 min

Servings: 6

Ingredients:

- Salt (1 teaspoon)
- Milk (1/4 cup)
- Pancetta slices, thin (12 pieces)
- Garlic cloves, chopped (3 pieces)
- Carrot, peeled, chopped finely (1 piece)
- Ground turkey (1 ½ pounds)
- Pasta sauce, tomato basil (3/4 cup)
- Breadcrumbs, panko, plain, crispy (1/2 cup)
- Onion, chopped finely (1/2 cup)
- Bell pepper, red, chopped finely (1/2 cup)
- Rosemary leaves, fresh, chopped finely (1 tablespoon)
- Pepper (1/2 teaspoon)
- Egg (1 piece)

Directions:

1. Preheat the air fryer at 375 degrees Fahrenheit.
2. Use foil to line a pan (15x10x1-inch).
3. Grease 12 muffin cups with butter.
4. Combine the breadcrumbs with milk and let sit for five minutes. Stir in the turkey, onion garlic, pepper, salt, rosemary, bell pepper, and carrot. Spoon mixture into the muffin cups.
5. Cover each muffin cup with pasta sauce (1 tablespoon) and pancetta slice (1 piece). Air-fry for eighteen to twenty-two minutes.

Conclusion

I hope this book was able to help you to understand the benefits of an Air Fryer and the basics on how to use it. The next step is to plan your meals and gather the ingredients. This appliance is easy to use and you will eventually get the hang of the process. Once you have tried several recipes, you can already start tweaking the ingredients to create variations or start making your own.

Enjoy the process of preparing your meals in a healthier way using this innovation when it comes to cooking.

The End

Thank you very much for taking the time to read this book. I tried my best to cover as many air fryer recipes as possible. If you found it useful please let me know by leaving a review on Amazon! Your support really does make a difference and I read all the reviews personally so can I understand what my readers particularly enjoyed and then feature more of that in future books.

I also pride myself on giving my readers the best information out there, being super responsive to them and providing the best customer service. If you feel I have fallen short of this standard in any way, please kindly email me at BarbaraTrisler@yahoo.com so I can get a chance to make it right to you.

I wish you all the best!

Index

42074196R00040

Printed in Poland
by Amazon Fulfillment
Poland Sp. z o.o., Wrocław